I0161057

Dedication

To my beautiful Gram, Janet, who taught me what it
means to be a righteous woman of God while
entrusting Him with our every struggle.

I love you!!

CONFIDENCE

Published by One Goal Productions Press

120 Chiefs Way, Suite 1 PMB 37 Pensacola, FL 32507

Book Tiffany Coverly to speak | Other Inquiries:

www.OneGoalProductions.org www.TiffanyCoverly.com

All rights reserved. No part of this book may be reproduced in any form by an electronic or mechanical means, including information storage and retrieval systems, without permission in writing from the publisher, except by a reviewer who may quote brief passages in a review. For permission, contact OneGoalProductions.org.

Cover & Layout Design, Tom Coverly

Author Photo, Tom Coverly

Editor, Mark Bringhurst

All Scripture quotations, unless otherwise noted, are taken from the Holy Bible, the Message version (MSG)®. Copyright © 1993-2002. All rights reserved by Eugene H Peterson.

© 2021 Tiffany Coverly

ISBN 978-1-7368106-0-6

eISBN 978-1-7368106-1-3

Printed in the United States of America

First Edition 2021

Confidence

CONTENTS

INTRODUCTION

Confidence. "Self-Esteem" "The feeling of self-assurance arising from one's appreciation of one's own abilities or qualities"

"For the Lord shall be your **confidence,** firm and strong, and shall keep your foot from being caught in a trap or some hidden danger"
Proverbs 3:26

You know, I used to struggle with **confidence** issues, and if I am completely honest......a little sneak peek into my tender heart would reveal, I still do. Funny, I believed that at some magic age of "Adulthood" (keeping in mind that I am 34, married, have children and still have yet to reach this "magical" stage, haha), that I would be everything that I was created to be and that lack-of-**confidence** would be one of the last nuisances interrupting my days. Good thing God's plans seem to be perpetually opposite of my own, otherwise I don't think I'd be writing this book. He has put such a sense of urgency on this message and I am so thankful you'll be reading it!!

"Many are the plans in a man's heart, but the Lord's purpose prevails" Proverbs 19:21

God sees us and accepts us right where we are, and His omnipotent and all-knowing outlook over things, puts us in the perfect hands to finish every good work that He has started within us. We are going to get exactly where we need to be; if we are trusting Him and allowing the work to transpire, whether we like it or not. GOOD NEWS!

I can assure you of one thing though; when God pressed it upon my heart to share with you through the words in this book that resonate so deeply within my own heart, I had never felt so self-assured in my entire life. These principles that I am on the verge of sharing with you, resound within me more as lessons than anything else. They are "gifts that keep on giving", and the truth is that our whole life is a God designed journey in which we continually learn to EMBRACE these principles, thus growing into the full fruition of everything God intended us to be. There is no mysterious formula, only God's leading. It honestly took me an overly impressive amount of time before I completely grasped and wrapped my head around this concept. That's me though, always taking the hard route that is generally less traveled, lol. Anyone else there with me? We simply cannot be transformed into righteousness and everything God created us to be, apart from God. Likewise, we cannot have complete **confidence** (or as I have heard it referred to as "Godfidence"), unless it comes from God. We simply cannot be without God, and everything essential that we are SO in desperate need of; comes from Him alone.

"I am the vine, you are the branches.
When you're joined with me and I with you;
the harvest is sure to be abundant, separated

you cannot produce a thing"
John 15:5

Pretty easy notion, right? Hasn't always been for me, and if I was to guess; it could very well be one of the essential reasons you are reading these words at this very moment. God lead you here and I am SO thankful that He did! If you are anything like me and oftentimes find yourself lacking **confidence,** are fearful, doubtful, feeling forgotten, depleting yourself of energy, requiring more growth in God but feeling guilty when you have trouble finding that time, feeling worthless INSTEAD of priceless; well CONGRATULATIONS, you are human....and I understand you more than you could ever know. Truly, I do! I have struggled with things that; frankly, I should have never have put myself through if I was consistently remembering where my internal strength comes from. We as women; regardless of age or the timeline in which you've been walking with Christ, can all relate. I; however, am here to display for you, just how normal you are. God handmade every single solitary part of your being, what makes you….YOU. EVERYTHING. He knows you, I mean REALLY knows you. Fully, completely & ENTIRELY. So much so, that He has bottled each and every tear that you've ever cried; you don't believe me, take a look…

> *"You keep track of my sorrows. You have*
> *collected all my tears in your bottle. You have*
> *recorded each one in your book"*
> *Psalm 56:8*

Ummm, I don't know about you, but I believe that to be pretty darn FANTASTIC! We have a nine year old daughter and just thinking about her sweet face; red puffy cheeks with tears streaming down, and I can tell you as much as it hurts my heart to see her cry, I have not bottled not one of them. The Bible also tells us that God knows distinctively EACH of the hairs on our head. (*Indeed, the very hairs on your head are numbered. Don't be afraid; you are worth more than many sparrows" Luke 12:7)* Okay, now Ladies; I don't know about you…..but I am an extreme SHEDDER.

My husband would be the first to vouch for me on this. I mean, I find my hair EVERYWHERE. The floor, caught in the vacuum, in my food, on my daughter's toast after I submerge it with peanut-butter, in my morning coffee (which is the absolute WORST!) so there is no telling you how much hair that I depart from on any given day. The new hairs that grow in their place; rest assured, they are counted too!!

Goodness gracious, our God is on FIRE! He's pretty amazing…...okay, ASTOUNDINGLY AMAZING!! The same God that handcrafted you, every intricate detail, has bottled your tears, counts each hair on your head and understands you entirely; has complete **confidence** in you, He has the perfect plan of attack against all these annoying **confidence** & self-esteem issues. Whew, this is great news; our God never puts us in a position where we have to "go it alone". God desires us to succeed while living joyfully and happily throughout our personal journey with Him, it is truly the desire of His heart. It would be an absolute shame to travel through our lives Ladies, and not fully develop into that "Powerhouse Warrior Woman of Christ" that has been waiting to burst out and take full residence within your heart and mind.

Do me a favor right quick. Put your hand on your chest and over your heart (go on, I am doing it right now too as I am writing, as I cannot ask you to do something I wouldn't do). She's in there, do you feel her heart beating inside of you? You know as well as I do what God is speaking to your heart at this exact moment. It's time. You've been lacking **confidence** and have been on what resembles a never-ending chase with your full potential for far too long; it's time, and through the Holy Spirit bringing these next chapters to life, He is going to show you and lead **you** specifically on your journey to a new beginning......

A journey to…**CONFIDENCE.**

CHAPTER ONE

WHO AM I?

"Now we look inside, and what we see is
that anyone united with the Messiah gets a
fresh start, is created new. The old is gone
& the new is here! Look!"
2 Corinthians 5:17

This past December, I was asked to come and speak for an annual Ladies Christmas Breakfast; I joyously accepted!! Something this particular local church holds each year, in which ladies would come to converse, laugh together, pray together, encourage each other; all while touring the lobby in which was FILLED from front to back with individuals sharing their love of creativity through crafts. The ladies arrived in the morning, shared breakfast together & then came to listen to worship & a word from God (this is where I enter in). I remember the week prior to the event; going through my talk and rehearsing down to the littlest details (I'm a little bit of a perfectionist at times, but only when it comes to myself), and in the midst of it all, I literally remember having the thought "How in the world am I going to do this?". Keeping in mind that I had previously spoken to women before and I had been performing and singing in worship for the majority of my life; this particular thought started a whirlwind of emotions of its own. Every ministry opportunity that we receive comes from God, He desires to use us to breakthrough to others, only in this specific moment I had forgotten a very pivotal truth; who I am in Christ. MY IDENTITY.

Nothing like putting out a heated & passionate flame of **confidence** in God, then allowing ourselves to not only forget our Identity; but forgetting all together, the authority we possess in Jesus name BECAUSE we are His precious Daughters'. He has chosen you; before you were ever born, and loves us unconditionally deeper than we'll ever be able to fathom in our minds. The Bible informs us; that because we've chosen Him, that when we unite with God during our salvation, we are made brand new. White as snow. Slate completely CLEAN. That's how the cookie crumbles ladies! It doesn't always appear this way or FEEL this way all of the time and at every given moment, but in the Spiritual realm…we've been given a new name. Who we appear to be versus who we actually are in Christ differs dramatically in God's eyes, and actually living out this Identity can prove to be challenging when we have our moments of depleted **confidence;** because we don't feel worthy of the authority that He has bestowed upon us.

Let me remind you, you are a Daughter of the King; a timeless treasure. In God's eyes you are His greatest masterpiece, and there is nothing that you could ever live out or say that would lead Him to have a change of heart. Girl, you are a Princess!! Hello! Go on with your bad self! Do you see how much authority and influence a Princess is actually graced with? She is held to the absolute highest of standards, but also given the world, EVERYTHING through this title. Allow me to remind you, that this beautiful and precious diamond does nothing to DESERVE her title, but it is simply received by being BORN into royalty. She is the Daughter of a King and because she is born into royalty, she is automatically endowed with the authority through her Father's name. She contains great **confidence** not because of who SHE is, but because of who her Father is. Ladies, you are royalty; through the royal bloodline of Christ, and the authority of Jesus name belongs to you!!

I had forgotten who I truly was, who God says that I am. My dear sweet husband was a tremendous encouragement also; as God uses those closest to us to speak through as well. In that moment it was very apparent to me the action that I needed to take. I craved **confidence** regeneration; the kind of **confidence** that can only be achieved through Christ's refreshing love. I got down on my knees and proceeded to cry out to my Heavenly Father. It was in the sacredness of my prayer;

the stillness of my spirit, and my surrendered heart, God's faithfulness bursted through, and reminded me of who I am in HIM. Who we are is so much more than our name, our family, our career, our hobbies, our dreams; it comes from a historic and irreplaceable lineage that embraces us and makes us new. It catapults us into a lifelong journey of developing and transforming into the very Woman that God created you to be; uniquely and pricelessly made.

> *"I praise you because I am fearfully*
> *and wonderfully made"*
> *Psalm 139:14*

It can be a downhill battle in your mind, and losing **confidence** oftentimes leaves us feeling like we're literally stagnant with our hands tied; but there are principles in which I utilize that God has placed on my own heart during a Spiritual attack of Identity theft:

1.) **Use the Authority-** As I so freshly spoke about; you have authority in Jesus name, and He wants you to utilize it! Praying in Jesus name, resisting the enemy in

Jesus name, and speaking blessings over your life, your family and your future in Jesus name. Just the picture I envision in my mind, the moment we release those words "In Jesus name"; demons fleeing, mountains shaking, battles within our hearts crumbling and walls falling at the sound. Literally, gives me goosebumps; seriously wish that you could see this as I am writing, INCREDIBLE!! Princess and Daughter of the King should be a daily mindset and our inherited authority of our Father's name, a never-ending blanket of protection covering our lives. The power is yours; God gave it to you, and no one can steal what belongs to you….especially not the enemy.

> *"Look, I have given you authority over*
> *all the power of the enemy, and you can walk*
> *among snakes and scorpions and crush them.*
> *Nothing will injure you."*
> *Luke 10:19*

2.) **God's Validation-** This right here. This is HUGE. In today's society it is no secret that seeking God's validation alone is not the desired or popular route to take. The world attempts to convince us that what others think about us matters greatly, and it doesn't. We seek value, self-validation and **confidence** through social media, movies, reality television, magazines, the opinion of other Women and I can assure you that indulging in this practice brings you to a startling realization of complete emptiness. I am seasoned in this particular area because I was this Woman, and there are moments that I; myself, am weak.....and I find myself hitting rock-bottom in this once again; dead-end scenario. I am going to be raw, real and transparent with you, I am guilty of this and there are times when I fail to remember that God's validation is the ONLY opinion that is able to restore me. Outside opinions may "feel" great at first, but they will always fall flat. I allow myself to care how others might think of me, or worse yet, judge me. I go about trying to mold myself into something more "desirable" according to the worlds idiotic standards; that's right, I said it. God created you, loves you unconditionally, desires you to be unique and flourish for who YOU are and not for what may be "popular" , "worldly acceptable", or who anyone else may be. We as Women especially, all have certain parts of our personalities or bodies that we wish were different; I'm right there with you Sister, but it's an outstandingly beautiful endeavor to travel with Jesus on the road to self-acceptance and **confidence**. His heart slowly becomes your heart, His thoughts start to become the first to engulf your mind in the moments of self-doubt; transforming your mind, renewing your Faith and creating such a "heavenly validation" in your spirit.

> *"I don't think the way you think. The way*
> *you work isn't the way I work"*
> *Isaiah 55:8*

3.) **Believe in Yourself-** "Words of Affirmation" is my love language. I've read through the book "The Five Love Languages"; learned so much about myself in the process, and affirmed love from my Husband and encouragement from others verbally, is the way in which I experience love to the fullest. This may be true for you too, or maybe one of the other four languages is more your cup of tea. In any case; words of affirmation and God's validation are only as good as the belief you have of them to be true. What I mean is; God could shower me with love, joy, acceptance and affirmation, but if I don't believe Him…..His words would easily fall to the waste side. Likewise, my sweet hubby could affirm me of his love, call me beautiful and assure me of the treasure I am in his life, but if I don't bring myself to believe it, what difference could it possibly create in my life? Now, this is the furthest thing from the truth and God has blessed me with the most outstanding Man of Christ. Ladies…..we need to BELIEVE in ourselves!! We don't just need to, we HAVE to. You must believe that you are worthy of an abundance of love, that you are truly a Daughter of the King & that you are AMAZING…..because you are INCREDIBLY AMAZING!! Consistently renewing your mind in these truths will erratically move your inner self and it will also begin to reflect on the outside too! A quote I just came across recently; fantastic, and I believe it applies perfectly "Wonder Woman is not a fictional character, Wonder Woman is a mindset! The subtitle on the cover of this book reads "Becoming the Powerhouse Woman of Christ that God created you to be", you are POWERFUL girl!! Believe in yourself, it's time to rock-it-out!! I want you to say it loud, right now "I AM A POWERHOUSE FOR JESUS CHRIST, THIS IS WHO I AM!" Little did you know, unbeknownst to you, this was an interactive book. God believes in you, I believe in you.....now, trust God and YOU believe in you!!

"For the Lord will be your confidence and will keep your foot from being caught"
Proverbs 3:26

4.) **Create a Mantra-** Speak Life. I am an encouraging advocate of speaking positive words and verses out-loud and speaking them over my life. Negative out and positive in. There isn't anything that can come up against the world and destroy the enemy like God's Word. Period. The Bible doesn't just come alongside and put out those flames of destruction; no, this living and breathing word demolishes their existence. There is no level of negativity that will not be destroyed when repetitive positivity is spoken and meditated upon. I need the Bible daily, I need to speak life daily; because if I am not consistently filled with God's Word and led by the Holy Spirit, there will always be an attempt from opposing forces to break through and take up residence in that sacred place. As difficult as it may be at times; to stop and speak truth over the negative ambushing our thoughts, it is essential and something God assists us with when we cry out to him.

> *"Set guard over my mouth, LORD; keep*
> *watch over the door of my lips"*
> *Proverbs 31:26*

Changing your thoughts and actions in the midst of those moments when you feel like giving up completely; connecting with God and allowing the Holy Spirit to lead you, now THAT is the game changer. You have the authority that has been given to you through Christ himself, you have the strength to change your mind, you DESERVE peace and joy......and now that you know who you ARE, you can do this!! God has every **confidence** in you.

Girl, let's get real. There are times when the enemy is right up in your face; I mean UP CLOSE AND PERSONAL, and all you have in that moment is enough strength to yell and scream out loud. Yell and scream God's truth, create that mantra or phrase that you use as a battle cry!! It's tough, so tough, but you CAN win and God has already got the victory.....tighten up those fists and punch Satan right where it hurts!! He's a punk and it's time to show him his place, under your feet in JESUS NAME! You've got this, because GOD*HAS*GOT*YOU.

CHAPTER TWO

DIVE INTO GOD'S WORD

"For the Word of God is alive and active. Sharper than any double-edged sword, it penetrates even to dividing soul and spirit, joints and marrow; it judges the thoughts and attitudes of the heart"

Hebrews 4:12

I am a runner. I love to run. Feeling the open air brushing against my face, heart beating at a faster pace; nothing like being able to utilize your body to become a stronger version of yourself. I can recall a time in particular; I went on a run in the early evening, my usual "Monday Night Run" down the long dirt-filled unpaved road just down the street from my home, and what I remember most was not how exhilarating it was, but the quick depletion of my energy that reared its ugly face way too soon. It was a type of exhaustion that I wasn't prepared for, but in hindsight was completely my fault. You see; I had forgotten the "golden rule" of exercise, STAYING HYDRATED. Up until this point, I had always remembered to grab myself a water bottle before sprinting out of the house & down the driveway; this evening was different, and I realized about 1/3 of the way through my structurally planned 3 mile run that I didn't have any water with me. I forgot it. I generally planned ahead to be hydrated, continue to stay hydrated while I run, and also re-hydrate once I'm finished. I couldn't very well successfully complete my 3 mile run without it; pushing myself through it would bring me to complete fatigue, and knowing my body.....that fatigue would most likely carry over into the next day. I had no choice than to turn around where I was in that moment, and head back to the place where I knew I could nurture my body once again. Home.

Isn't that how it goes though? Comparing this to our time in God's Word. We plan it out; something unexpected interrupts or happens that takes away from that sacred block of time with God, and a lot of times it gets forgotten. I know that I have personally struggled at times with making time for Jesus; when I know it SHOULD be the most important part of my day. It isn't until we are in a situation where we need God's help or perhaps the enemy strikes and before you know it, you're smack dab in the middle of spiritual warfare. I can tell you one thing; with complete CERTAINTY.....those mornings that I devote my mind, my spirit, and my heart completely to God and diving into His word, are the most integral parts of my day. That sacred interaction with God sets the tone for every interaction, restores my **confidence,** prepares me for the enemies attacks, fixes my mind on all of the amazing blessings in my life, and fills my cup to the brim with joy, peace and happiness. Our bodies are made of almost entirely of water; we NEED water to survive and can only stay alive for a certain amount of time without it. God created us; we NEED God, and we can only get by without Him for a certain amount of time before it becomes too much. Truth be told, God created us to need Him ALL of the time; just like we cannot deprive our bodies of water, we cannot deprive ourselves of God and His word. Being devoid of God's word and struggling along from day to day is not how He planned it out for you, and just like you need food and water to survive; for your body to run properly, our spirits simply cannot breathe and grow sufficiently without The Bible. Sure, we could continue on each day without it, but trust me when I say that you WILL experience the difference. If you haven't ever experienced the difference of God's Word in your life compared to your life without, I recommend that you try it today, don't waste another second. It feels so refreshing within you when you really begin to drink it all in and ask God to help you grow and understand with every verse that floods your mind.

The more you indulge into this juicy book of breathing life (Yes, I call it Juicy; it's an amazing book, and the contents are incredible when consumed daily), God will speak to you. This isn't a competition on how much you can read to be a "good Christian" or how much you can memorize at any one setting; it's about a relationship, a heart change....a LIFE change. You dive into God's Word daily and it begins to consume you; your thoughts, your actions, and it prepares you to handle anything and everything that is brought before you during each day. It doesn't need to be boring; I don't read the Bible for hours every day, and I spend more time talking with God like I do my best friend.....and He reveals little nuggets of gold found in scripture that will knock your socks off!! I kid you not! It happens for me, continues to happen and just as long as I am seeking Him, He will always be speaking. God's absolute favorite moments to speak to me are in the middle of the night; when I am sleeping, and He enjoys waking me up to give me such pivotal things, that I MUST get out of bed to write them down. hehe. He wants to speak to you too! Did you know that God has things that He desires to reveal to you and ONLY YOU; secrets that you couldn't even fathom just yet, and when He does.....it literally feels as though you've won the lottery. You know; without a doubt, that God is talking directly to your heart, and there isn't another touch of love quite like His. You cannot have a successful relationship with Jesus without it.

A little something I might have stolen from my amazing Husband; for each day of the month I read the corresponding chapter within Proverbs, and then I pray about what God would reveal to me to apply to my everyday life. The Proverbs are filled with wisdom, good sense and incredible leading on so many life topics; God will lead you from there. Everything will begin to change, I promise you. I'm a huge journal writer, so on most days I will either post an encouraging message on Social Media if God leads me to do so, or I jot down the messages He brings to my heart meant for just me to be aware of; either way, God WILL speak to you if you ask Him to with an eager and open heart. You cannot learn how to properly achieve success in running a machine that wasn't created by you; you almost always need the Instruction Manual, and just as the Instruction Manual is to the well-oiled machine.....so is The Bible for the incredible **confident** Y★O★U.

Just as I mentioned earlier; this is an interactive book, and we are going to do this together. So, grab your Bible (or tap on your "Bible" App), head to Proverbs and choose the chapter that corresponds with today's date (for me that would be February 19th), and read the chapter. Commit. You can do this!! Once you are done; write down your favorite scripture within the text on the spaces provided below and ask God to reveal to you, what He will. Let these words penetrate your heart like never before and listen for His sweet words within your spirit. I'm going to be doing this with you, you GO GIRL!!

CHAPTER THREE

REMOVING THE NEGATIVE

"Summing it all up, friends, I'd say you'll do best by filling your minds and meditating on things that are true, noble, reputable, authentic, compelling, gracious-the best, not the worst; the beautiful, not the ugly; things to praise, not things to curse"
Philippians 4:8

This is honestly the last chapter of this book to be written (and it's chapter 3 to you in your reading). It may be the shortest but I promise it's quite action packed! I felt like this was the best place to insert it. Yes, right here. It was a pondering thought previously and has once again come to the forefront of my mind. I believe it is truly important to address; as simple as it is, it is VITAL to; because in a world filled with negativity, filth, temptation and addiction. We are called in God's word to be living the exact opposite to these things. I want to expand a slight bit more than just what we are thinking; as it reads in the verse above, I also want to concentrate on other factors in your everyday life that can be affecting your well-being and **confidence.** We should definitely be filling our minds with God's word each day, thinking only things that would be pleasing to the Father, but also at times it calls us to put space between ourselves and negative individuals.

God calls us to love others; which I am NOT speaking against here, but what I mean is distancing yourself from the people within your life that literally suck the life out of you. When you are with them; negativity spews from their mouth, discontent is completely evident, and once you part with them you feel like you've been hit by a truck. Okay,

okay….maybe we won't go that far. I would be willing to bet that each and every one of you ladies has AT LEAST one person like this in your life. It can be a family member, friend, coworker, etc. As I said, God calls us to love them, pray for them and be KIND to them, but nowhere in the Word of God does it say "Thou shalt be a doormat". Some of you are like "Whoa, HOMEGIRL IS LAYING IT OUT" LOL! Yes, because I truly believe it needs to be said; because I know the feeling that these people have induced into my life, and it can be extremely stressful. Honest truth, it sucks the life out of you! God does not desire for you to be feeling this way & He certainly doesn't call you to consistently be around someone that depletes you of your **confidence** and positivity. They have the power to plant a negative seed in you, that could potentially take YEARS to remove, depending on how much time you spend with them. You can distance yourself from them, love them and continue to pray for them; and still be well within how Christ would desire for you to be acting. Ladies, I've had these individuals in my life, and I did take my own advice in this; IT'S SO

REFRESHING. What happens when you distance yourself from them, is that God is able to bring individuals into your life to BLESS you, PRAY for you, and BE THERE for you when you need them. It's an amazingly beautiful thing and these ladies have become my very best friends. These blessed individuals truly and genuinely care about you, your well-being, your relationship with God and they LOVE to cheer you on. IMAGINE THAT! If you were waiting for a sign on what to do, this is your sign; it's time to get your sanity back! I am always going to keep it raw and real with you. Let's not try and sugarcoat this, because when it's happening to you, it's no "sweet" matter. It potentially leaves you feeling trapped because you want to be a woman of God you know you're supposed to be, but you also don't enjoy being around the negativity. A lot of times they are fellow Christians, which makes everything that much more confusing. PRAY GIRL, pray about it and ask God to help!!

It will eventually begin to make you feel like you aren't somehow good enough; because everything you try to do, won't ever be decent enough for them. They will always find a way to bring negative out of even the most POSITIVE of situations. They generally never admit when they are wrong, and they don't like to apologize for anything. Then, if you aren't careful, you'll find yourself starting to sound like them at times....that is when you know that something isn't right, because it goes against what God desires for you in Philippians 4:8. I will tell you; ALWAYS, pray about this before proceeding. I would never tell you to distance yourself from someone that God has called you to be serving or witnessing to in some way; because I do know that God can oftentimes bring lessons through those times. If it's been on your mind, go to God and ask Him what you should do going forward. He sees your stress, your frustration, your depleted energy, and He CARES how you feel; He knows what's going on. God will always lead you in the right direction, and He will show you how to go about it.

The negative can be coming in the form of a person or persons of course, but there are also negative circumstances, addictions, daily rituals that can also hinder you in your growth and steal your **confidence.**

I know that as you are reading this at this very moment, you each have at least one particular thing you can think of at this time; something most likely God has been placing on your heart, and today He is bringing it forth once again to remind you that it's something that you can either live without or He wants to help you manage it. Whatever it may be; don't let it ruin your progress and what God is trying to do within your life, because the only person it's hurting is you. You deserve to be happy, you deserve peace and joy, and most importantly **confidence.**

CHAPTER FOUR

STOP LISTENING TO THE ENEMY

"The thief comes only to steal and kill and
destroy; I have come that they may have life
and have it to the full"
John 10:10

I f I had a quarter for each and every time the enemy filled my mind with thoughts of confusion, insecurity, worry, fear and anxiety; I'd literally be the most wealthy individual on the planet. I am sure of it! I have allowed the enemy to steal my **confidence** on FAR too many occasions. Choosing not to listen to such nonsense on a daily basis is by far easier said than done, trust me. It is and always will be a struggle, IF you allow it to be. Some of you are like "Wait, I actually have a choice?" and don't worry, I know exactly how you feel and I relate. I feel so blessed that I've come such a long way (with God leading), against the enemy, but rest assured; I have a very long way to go. It doesn't seem to matter with age; as far as his attacks lessening, it remains the same. He just comes up with new ammunition daily. PUNK.

God has given us His Word, His promises and prayer as powerful weapons against Satan and his disgusting schemes. He is truly a PUNK. To put it into perspective; there is NEVER a time that the enemy stops plotting against you. Girl, the Bible tells us that his desire is to STEAL, KILL & DESTROY you and everything good in your life. He's like an invisible killer!! I mean, let's pause for a moment; reread that last sentence, and genuinely allow it to set in your spirit. Satan means business, and he's in the business to ensure that you NEVER live the full and beautiful life that Christ has prepared for you. He cares NOTHING about the quality or longevity of your life. He knows no love, no compassion, no truth; just lies and deceit.

We read in James 1:17 that "every good and perfect gift is from above" and Satan will always be right there, ready to pounce on every blessing that enters your life. It's time that we use the resources we've been given by our Heavenly Father himself and FIGHT. Let's say you had taken the time to plan a very special visit to the zoo with your family; you hear a news story a few days prior that the animals had escaped and were roaming all over inside the zoo, what would you do? Would you still decide to bring your family, your children to the zoo unarmed, allowing anything and everything to devour you and your entire family? OF COURSE YOU WOULDN'T! So then, if the enemy roams around like a roaring lion seeking to devour us, why should we not take the exact same precautions? Satan doesn't sleep when we sleep, he doesn't get lazy when we feel lazy, he doesn't care deeply about things like we do; his existence revolves around waiting for you to "forget" he's there or slip in your daily grind, and he'll be right there to meet you with the pot roast of terror he's been cooking up and waiting to serve to you.

Satan absolutely hates YOU, yes YOU! Of course

it's not good to overestimate his power, but on the other hand it's more of a daily happenstance that we FORGET just how much more power we have over him in Jesus name!! There is NOTHING that he can stand against when you are bringing in the name of Jesus, spending time in God's presence. GIRL, he is going to try and get all up in your face & in your business and we need to stand firm; shoulders back, and kick his little booty out da door!! He isn't going to leave kindly either. In the name of Jesus; he must flee, but rest assured that he'll be back again....each time bringing more fire power in hopes of destroying you little by little in each consecutive round. It reminds me of one of my absolute favorite movies, Rocky IV. Yes, ladies, I love this movie and I am a huge dork, so it goes hand in hand. Trust me here. If you haven't seen it; allow me to give you a quick synopsis. Rocky Balboa (Sylvester Stallone) is a world renowned boxer, set to face Captain Ivan Drago (Dolph Lundgren) in order to keep his title as world champion and also avenge the death of his best friend Apollo Creed, in which Drago defeated and laid to rest (we'll say) during a previous fight. Now

MONTHS prior to the fight they show you the training that both of these men take themselves through in hopes of defeating the other. Now, they have Drago enduring some pretty crazy training; some things in which he hasn't ever done before while training, all in hopes of defeating the GREAT Rocky Balboa. But then, over on the opposite end, you have my boy Rocky training; tale as old as time, back to the basics.....KNOWING that he can TRUST what has brought him success and **confidence** previously. He isn't looking to perform any "parlor tricks" and almost kill himself in the process of training to win this fight, because he trusts completely in what has worked in the past. If you haven't seen the movie, you'll have to. I will fill you in on the ending (because I kind of have to in order to prove my point, lol), but Rocky prevails. He defeats Drago and remains the world champion. In the same way as Rocky sticking to what he knows to protect and train him, we have access to the same. There isn't a fancy way to defeat the enemy; the name of Jesus and scripture is THE way to defeat him. You turn it over to God; keep things simple, and the enemy will be defeated. News flash that you can always remind him of too, it's your triumph to OWN girl!! Put your gloves up girl and pop him in the face! BOOM!

Sometimes it's easier to just allow the enemy to get the best of us, to give into his lies, to breathe life into the insecurities; to deplete our **confidence.** There are moments when we feel weak, defeated and unable to move forward. The moments you feel that if anyone knew what was going on, they'd be sure to judge you. Those moments where you're down on your knees, face flat on the floor, crying out to God; when your mind tells you that what the enemy is feeding you MUST be real. It makes you feel worthless, invaluable and unwanted.....ladies, I want you to know that you don't have to feel that way! You DON'T deserve to live like that and you can escape that little "personal prison" that the enemy has you all caught up in. It can make you feel crazy at times. I get it and I've been there!! By submitting to God in those moments; giving it all to Him, and telling the enemy "TAKE A HIKE", he has no choice but to adhere to your request. Let me remind you; you are a Daughter of the King, crying out to her Daddy, and He desires to keep you safe. Satan stands NO CHANCE on that sacred ground in those sacred moments. He cowers in complete fear of the Father and of YOU Daughter; utilizing your royal right within the Kingdom of God. I have no doubt in my mind that if we actually were able to observe what goes on in those moments around us in the spirit realm, it would be beyond our comprehension (and pretty darn spiffy in my opinion). Our God wants to protect us and the enemy doesn't have to hinder us if we don't allow him.

The attacks are not something that you have to allow, so don't. DON'T. EVER. Refuse to allow him such wiggle room in your life, your mind, your heart, your thoughts and your **confidence.** Break those chains completely and be completely confident that your Heavenly Father is right behind you; smiling down, and proud of your fight to keep your peace and joy. Speak out the Word of God each and every time that he throws his nasty lies your way. The Bible tells us that if you "Submit yourself to God, Satan will flee"and that is the truth; he has absolutely no choice in the matter.

Satan stands no chance against you, so don't give him anymore of that luxury. His plans will burn to the ground when you are standing on the word of God, it's time to light that match and set fire to his lies in your life!

CHAPTER FIVE

NO JUDGEMENT

"Do not judge, or you too will be judged. For the same way you judge others, you will be judged, and with the measure you use, it will be measured to you"
Matthew 7:1-2

The CRAZY part about this particular chapter; my book is nearly finished, and this past 15 day stretch on the road brought this topic to my mind & heart. Typically, it should be a no brainer; right, but God has been placing it so very tenderly within my spirit (okay, He basically let me know that it WOULD be a chapter in my book, lol), but the reasoning behind it was something completely new and refreshing that He has shown me in order to show you. God tells us in the Bible that if we judge others, we will be judged; and in the same intensity that we are giving that judgement. I don't know about you, but....eeeeeeek!! The thought of that just sounds horrible and literally makes me want to always be more mindful of judgements that I may be passing or might be passing upon others in the future. Now, I know what some of you may be thinking "Well, I certainly don't judge others". But, if we are really and truly honest with ourselves, we ALL do ladies. I'm right there with you and it just seems to be at its worst during those moments when my **confidence** is wearing thin. You see, social media doesn't help AT ALL; which; by the way I will touch base on in a later chapter, because this is such a separate entity within itself. It's the way the "worldly" world functions unfortunately, and even though we may be women of Christ always striving for better, we fall victim as it sucks us in, in such a sneaky little way. It's almost as though it captivates our hearts at times, doesn't it; like a weird little "safe zone".

So, allow me to take you through the process of

judging another person, a lot of times in our case ladies; another woman. It's a pretty self-explanatory step by step "judging program" that we use within us, but there is another aspect of it that you might not have ever looked at before. So, you've spotted your victim (just play along), you see her and you notice something in particular about the way that she looks, the way she's dressed, her personality or maybe even what she is doing, and BAM…..it happens. Our alter-judgmental ego rears it's little ugly head. You see, because it is generally NEVER the individual as a whole, it's always something more specific, and frequently it comes out more because of **confidence** and jealousy issues. Okay, so this chapter is a deep one, and it will cause you to look inside yourself; just like it did me. It's a "spiritual" love tap from God we'll call it; makes it sound a little less daunting and uninviting. SO, you've now made the judgement and you feel as though it makes you feel better, better than HER. In reality my sweet ladies; there is something going in within your spirit in that moment that is extremely detrimental to your growth and **confidence.** A lot of times, we judge in our own minds just so no one else can hear, but sometimes I think we forget that God hears EVERYTHING. He watches us and observes us as we give into it.

You see; with each passed judgement on someone else, a little part of your spirit is suffering. Now, we don't see it at first because we don't even realize the seed that we are planting inside of ourselves when we do it. This isn't a seed of love, hope, joy, **confidence** and it certainly isn't HOLY. It's like an addiction; you don't see a problem at first, and then over time it starts taking a toll on every aspect of your body and life; then one day it has the potential to completely destroy you. I am about to get as raw and real with you as I ever have been; you ready? Ladies, I have suffered with lack of **confidence** for years, and my judgmental skills at times are RIGHT ON PAR, and I don't mean that in a flattering way. Am I ashamed? During a time that I honestly didn't even realize what I was doing because it happened so naturally; yes, but now I know better and God is HEALING those places. Jealousy and lack of **confidence** happen; they do, and you aren't alone. Let me repeat that, GIRL YOU ARE NOT ALONE!

BUT, they are signals to you, that there is a deeper issue at hand. God has been teaching me; that when I go about judging someone, it simply means there are places in my heart and spirit that need HEALING. So, I have literally been taking a deep breath each time I may even THINK of passing judgement; stopping, and asking God to reveal to me what is bringing up these feels within me when it comes to this particular individual, and THEN asking Him to begin healing me in those places that I cannot see. It's an amazingly BEAUTIFUL (and painful at times) process, and it is just what I needed. I then knew God had taken me on a journey that He wanted me to share with YOU. This is NEVER to make you feel ashamed; on the contrary, I want to help you.....because I GET you, and because God's GOT you. Everyone has a story, victories, brokenness and heartache; a living and breathing human being with a beating heart, just like you. It was definitely a revelation when God brought this to me in the way He did; He's so good like that, displaying what we NEED in ways that we can fully comprehend and ACCEPT it.

None of us are perfect and the Lord is forever working on us and through us to bring us into full fruition of His plan for us. You should never feel condemned in this process; that would be the enemy, but a constant **confidence** in God's love and understanding for you. That has to be the most downright amazing thing through all of us, He walks with us completely through our brokenness, being judgmental and comprehends perfectly what it is that we need and His desire is for you to be full of love, joy, healing and **confidence.**

CHAPTER SIX

HEARING GOD'S VOICE

"Call to me and I will answer you,
and will tell you great and hidden things that
you have not known"
Jeremiah 33:3

I remember growing up in church; as my grandparents took my brother and I all throughout our younger years and into our teenage years, and the topic of "hearing God's voice" was a very much something that was frequently discussed. I also remember feeling like it was something that was so impossible to achieve. I honestly feel like we put too much pressure on ourselves and feel less than worthy at times to actually hear from God. It's like a constant "If you follow these 5 steps" along with also reading the articles on "Is it REALLY God you're hearing from?" Ugh. Doesn't it just make you feel tired thinking about it? It can deplete you of your **confidence** and make you feel so undeserving of hearing God's voice. The funniest and most blessed thing about it is, it is actually quite simple to hear from God. Whew!! Wait, what?!........

Let me share a story with you of something that just recently happened to me this week when my daughter and I were shopping at Walmart down here in Pensacola. I needed a dressing room because I had a few things that I wanted to try on and there were two women working at that time in the women's department, but for some reason neither of them could let me into a fitting room and they had to call another young lady to come help me. Over five minutes went by and I was still waiting for this young girl and also a dressing room. She finally arrived and was very apologetic that she was not there sooner and I could tell by their faces and their demeanor toward her, that her coworkers were not very happy with her. I assured her that it was okay and that it was no big deal at all. Now, I have a tattoo of a beautiful sunflower on my right shoulder along with words "blessed is she who believes", derived from Luke 1:45 " blessed is she who believes that the Lord will fulfill the promises that he has spoken to her" she immediately saw it and began asking me about it and complimenting me on how beautiful and bright it was. She told me about how sunflowers are her absolute favorite flower (which are also mine as well and hence the reason I have one tattooed on my shoulder). She then began telling me of how jealous she was that I had such a nice summer tan and that she had not had a chance to work on hers because she was inside working. Something in me knew something about this young girl in this moment and I could not quite explain it but I knew that God was speaking to my spirit as I was talking to her, she was screaming for love and validation through the things that she was saying & I am not really sure if she realized she was doing it. She was genuinely so sweet and kind and also made conversation with my daughter as I was using the dressing room. By the end of it I thanked her so much for helping us and we went about our way. It wasn't until we got home that immediately I heard God talking to me and placed this young girl on my heart. It came across so clear as day and completely unmistakable that it was His voice. I did not have to do anything to provoke it and I did not ask him to speak to me in this way but He knew exactly what He wanted to say in that moment and He definitely let it rip!! You see, when God wants to talk to you; He is going to talk to you, and believe me when I tell you this.... in moments like that you will NEVER mistake the sound of His voice in your spirit. NEVER. God placed on my heart in that moment that the young girl needed to know just how kind and special she was; how beautifully and wonderfully she was made. After discussing it with my daughter we came up with a way to make her feel very special. The very next day we visited a local florist and bought her two of the most beautiful sunflowers and took them to Walmart in hopes that she would be there working. She WAS. God already knew she would be there. I told her about how God had placed her on my heart and that He does not do those things without a purpose. I also let her know that even though my tattoo may have been beautiful and bright, her personality and kindness is the true beauty and brightness that draws individuals' hearts to happiness. My little girl looked her in the face and told her "thank you for your kindness", and then proceeded to hand her the sunflowers. She told us that she had been having the worst day but now it was turned around and that it was going to make her cry. I didn't really know if she was a young woman of faith but I did write the scripture Psalm 139:14 at the bottom of the card tied to the flowers. You see, I hadn't been doing anything special at all to hear God's voice or for Him to use me in the way that He did, BUT He did!! He will speak to you too. You don't need any five step program or to be doing anything special or more than the next person, but just loving him with everything that you have, staying in His word, and that is all that He requires. To sit there and analyze trying to figure out if you are hearing His distinct voice, is like trying to figure out if you have really heard your favorite song before. It doesn't make any sense for you to do that because you know your favorite song, and you've heard it so many times before. You KNOW it, because no other song sounds close to it. On this day; and generally every day, it is this easy to hear from God....TRULY. I feel like the church sometimes makes it so much more complicated than it needs to be. Yes, I said it.

I do agree; however, that there are times that it is more difficult to hear from God, but He is ALWAYS willing to speak to us. The times that I am down and out, totally messed up & a big blubbering mess (I mean snot everywhere and crying like a baby) are the moments I hear Him the most clear. CRAZINESS. The things that you care about, He cares about. When you are sad and upset, He is sad and upset. I've come to find out; that if you want to hear God's voice, all you have to do is ASK Him. Believe me, once you hear His voice.....you'll never mistake it again. I used to think I was mistaken and felt confused if what I was hearing was actually the voice of God, but then I soon realized that it was an issue with me not openly listening. The moment when your spirit becomes calm, even in the midst of chaos and you hear even the slightest whisper. We all have those moments when we've messed up and feeling like there is NO WAY God is going to talk to me right now "Girl, I just acted a FOOL"! He ALWAYS desires to speak to us. It is a friendship too, remember and God wants to be our best friend. I know that if I didn't allow my best friend to speak to me after speaking to her; she'd be wondering what was going on? We have to be willing to listen; once that desire is there, it's an open 2 way street ladies. Talk to Him. Ask Him questions. He will talk back, girl. Trust me.

God will never leave you nor forsake you, and there isn't anything that could possibly cause Him to walk out on you and never return. He's ALWAYS there to forgive, to be present when you call on Him. He desires to talk with you SO MUCH!! There have been times; if I'm being raw and real, that I, myself have tried to hide myself from God because the shame of something I had done was so great. BUT, it's kind of like this.....remember that groovy little game you used to play with friends or siblings as a child; you know the one where you go and hide, and someone counts down until it's time to come and attempt to find you? YES! Hide and Seek, hehe....that's the one! Bingo! Yahtzee!

It's a lot like that. We will be off attempting to "hide" and God is already on the way to come find us, and watch our faces when He does. There may have been times when hiding as a kid or you trying to find someone else, that you weren't always successful in this and you ended up having to yell out "I can't find you, you have to come out" Well, with God; He will always find you. ALWAYS. That still small voice once again whispers to us "FOUND YOU!" and once we eventually get over that initial shame or hatred for ourselves, we lift our eyes up to our Father, to hear His voice say once again "I love you my child, I am so in love with you, you make me smile, and I am so proud of you". This moment ALWAYS makes me cry, always....because when we really think about how undeserving we are and how GLORIOUS He is to love us so much, it's simply incredible.

Be ready and willing to hear, my dear sister. The voice of God in your life will be nothing short of a miraculous miracle; His beautiful words are like food for our heart and spirit, and one touch from God can change your whole life. Pray, speak, listen. The Lord is so close to you when you speak, He hears every word and He is ready to speak freely to YOU!

CHAPTER SEVEN

FORGIVENESS

"I can do all things through Christ
who strengthens me"
Philippeans 4:13

Believe it or not; out of all 13 chapters in my book, this is one of the last chapters to be started. I have completed or am close to completing every other chapter, and this is completely peculiar to me; or is it? Good ole forgiveness, hello old friend. If I'm being entirely honest, I may be harboring some UNforgiveness within my heart; festering around, and trying to take away my **confidence.** If you are also being honest with yourself.....you may be too (or have been in "the land of unforgiveness" before). They say that if you wait until you are COMPLETELY ready for something, you most likely will never be fully ready; until you take that plunge. Forgiveness can sometimes feel like a "polar" plunge; as it can lead to a feeling of vulnerability, and sometimes that vulnerable state can get quite cold out there on that ledge. But, it is EXACTLY where you need to be; so JUMP off that ledge.

We have all heard the saying "Un-forgiveness doesn't hurt the person in which you are holding it towards, but in reality it's only hurting you". Now, I realize that some of you quite possibly have never heard this statement until now. Some of you, this may be the only epiphany that you need to move past something you've been struggling with, but if you're anything like me, I am still trying to grasp this concept completely in my own mind and heart. Do I enjoy torturing myself? HEAVENS NO! But sometimes it just feels safer, like we somehow have control over that person or persons; leaving them powerless. THIS, my dear ...is the TRAP.

Let me spell it out for you (LITERALLY)

T: Torture, the kind of torture that implants fear, doubt & worry into all aspects of your life. You've heard or maybe even seen in movies, the crazy form of Chinese Torture. The slow and frustrating death because you just cannot take it anymore. You feel dead inside, you feel nothing and you also feel like it will never end. TORTURE, this is what unforgiveness becomes. It is not only torture for your mind, but for body, heart and soul. It can literally destroy you.

R: Relationships: When you hold unforgiveness against someone, it will affect every other relationship in your life. Yes, EVERY other relationship. It causes mistrust in every important relationship you currently have, because you couldn't stand someone committing such ridiculousness toward you once again. Our brains cannot always decipher hurt, as it pertains to those in our life; so while we are angry with one individual; a lot of times someone else receives the brunt of that anger. Case and point, a husband and wife....it happens all the time, not being gracious with our spouse because of something someone may have said or did to you earlier that day. It is so easy to harbor anger, guilt, sadness from unforgiveness that we allow it to become a part of how we treat others in our relationships. Just remember, the good and loving individuals in your life are NOT the person or persons who have hurt you; as hard as it can be to trust going forward, God can give you the strength to do so.

A: Assumption: Unforgiveness causes you to just assume things about people that may not even be true. You cannot fully love and accept people when you are harboring unforgiveness in your heart. It gives you a jaded view of everyone you come into contact with. Those "rose colored" glasses become muddied and brown. ICK. It comes from that place of being hurt, being scared. If you are assuming the worst of others, then you will definitely be assuming the worst of yourself and that leads to the total destruction of **confidence** in your life.

P: Presence: Unforgiveness keeps you literally LOCKED in the past, unable to move forward and grow. Picture yourself in the driver's seat of your car; now imagine yourself looking up into your rearview mirror, and seeing everything going on behind you. Now, I want you to picture yourself hitting the gas pedal (while still looking in ONLY your rearview mirror) and feel the car begin to accelerate. How do you feel? Do you have **confidence** in driving forward without being able to see what is right in front of you? My prediction is that your answer is NO. BUT, if you take your eyes and fix them on the windshield and what is on the horizon, you can be sure that you'll get to where you need to go. You HAVE to let it go. You HAVE to forgive, so that you can move forward with your life and everything God has for you. God cannot give you His blessings if you are living in the past......because He doesn't live in the past. You cannot possibly get to the next level when you're trying so hard to frantically hold onto the step previous. You are literally holding yourself in contempt, in BONDAGE. Just like you cannot read the end of the story if you keep re-reading the same chapter over and over again.....how boring. How ludicrous. But we do it, don't we ladies. I do relate with you, but it is time to let go.

I want you to know ladies; as I am writing this out now, I am writing from experience. When the ones that are supposed to love and protect you, simply hurt you or walk away. I have felt these things, I know these things and I am currently STRUGGLING with these very things RIGHT AS WE SPEAK. I am not afraid to be raw, real and honest. It is what I (we) do going forward that builds our character as women in Christ; just like everything else, we DON'T have to go through the process of forgiveness alone. I honestly believe that God structured forgiveness this way for a reason; He knows that we cannot possibly do it without Him. Sure, we can verbally forgive from the outside; just so everyone can hear (even hear ourselves say it), but if we look inside the heart.....without God's help.....it can a lot of times linger and become greater than it needs to be. Forgiveness; for some, will be a one time thing, but if you are anything like me....it's a DAILY thing. A daily choice to forgive, sometimes the same person or situation over and over again. God is so gracious about entering in, right there in those moments and saving us. It never gets old to Him, He never feels nagged or frustrated, He feels PROUD that you are choosing to forgive regardless of the pain you are feeling. The very last thing on your mind and heart is forgiveness in those moments, but it's exactly what God desires for you. It's how He loves us. It is how He so freely forgives us. Life is so very short to be bitter, resentful and unforgiving of others', truly. It makes our bodies sick, our minds sick, everything about us becomes ill when we hold onto these things. The Bible literally tells us this about holding grudges from unforgiveness

"Work on getting along with each other
and with God. Otherwise, you'll never get
so much as a glimpse of God"
Hebrews 12:15.

You see, unforgiveness also puts a rift between you and God. It's time to let it go; give it to God, and be FREE. Even if it takes multiple attempts to let go, do it......get your life back girl!! God will handle everything else. That doesn't always mean that when forgiveness takes place within you; that everything will be completely better between you and the other person or persons. No, it means that you will be able to REALLY breathe again. It means that each time that person or persons enter your mind that your spirit and heart remain at peace, stealing away no **confidence** from your bitterness that USED to reside there.

CHAPTER EIGHT

"LET YOUR FAITH BE BIGGER THAN YOUR FEAR"

"Be strong and courageous, do not be afraid or tremble at them, for the Lord your God is the one who goes with you. He will not fail or forsake you"
Deuteronomy 31:6

They say that courage is not the absence of fear, but the realization that something else is more important than the fear. Jesus didn't say that it would be easy, but He does say that it will always be worth it. Putting our complete trust and faith in God through all things is definitely what He desires, but never are we supposed to expect that all worry, doubt & fear will completely diminish from our minds when we do. It is all about having the **confidence** to let your faith be bigger than your fears. Growing into a new dimension of our **confidence** and relationship with Christ; almost always requires a new level of courage and uncomfortability, but by facing your fears.....you come out better than you were before.

There have been so many instances in my life that I've failed to grow in certain areas as fast as I could or should have; because I allowed myself to be afraid and retreat back to my "safe" zone. Being in a safety zone isn't trusting Jesus, but choosing to stay in the same place that is familiar. I get it, it's the same that you've always known; it works for you, and it's so cozy. The crazy thing I had to come to realize was that my REAL safe zone was in Jesus ALONE. Believe me when I tell you, that God WILL bring you out of that comfort zone; whether we go peacefully or through a painful process (that is unfortunately the path I've taken far too many times, but He DOES bring it all together for our good! Whew!) Now I would never sit here and tell you that I have it all figured out, because I don't, in fact......I still to this very day allow myself to put fear before faith. Like I can somehow control the situation with fear, when all it's doing is demolishing my spirit and my ability to grow in Christ. I recently released a self-titled debut EP; I am also a singer too, and I wrote a song and the very first part of the lyrics go like this. *I don't know about you, but I've got a little feeling, trying to get ahead of God, like I've got a reason."* Let me fill you in on a little secret ladies; because I've learned the hard way, that there is NEVER a reason to get ahead of God. NEVER. Unless you enjoy yourself face down on the pavement, lol. FOR REAL. Far too many times I've found myself in this place, so of course I had to put it in a song. God has this HUGE beautiful plan for all of us, but fear puts so many roadblocks in the way; luckily we aren't able to ruin God's plans in the process. I am sure though; in these moments, that God looks down on us and wonders why we put ourselves through it. Fear stems from things we've been through that have caused deep seeded hurts; that in turn create these "protection barriers" in which we throw up every time we feel like we need to feel shielded. Instead of using the shield of faith as the Bible calls us to bring up each and every day, we choose the shield of fear. Does it make sense; no, but we choose this route because we feel like we can only trust ourselves in those moments, because why would we hurt ourselves? God would never want to hurt us, but when we choose fear; our hearts and minds tell us that no one (not even God) can protect us. When what we are doing is directly hurting ourselves.

I am an author, writer, singer, but I am also a speaker. I get stage fright at times, simply put. It happens to me every time. I never seem to get dry-mouth at any other time in my life EXCEPT for when I am about to go on stage. My knees also get weak too. I've read articles about this happening to famous individuals in movies and even live TV; craziness! These are definitely moments that I've learned to have to let God take over, I have no other choice, otherwise I might fall over on stage. LOL. Before I head up on stage, I always say a prayer and I generally ask God to remove my fear and replace it with Faith, and everything ends up completely fine. It's moments like these in our life that God uses to

FORCE us to rely on Him, and I am so glad that He is completely reliable! WHEW!

If I am completely honest with you, I will share a very private part of my heart with you. As a 34 year old woman, I still find myself in this area more often than not. I know exactly who I need to run to; our Heavenly Father, yet I choose trusting myself over trusting God. There are literally times that I cannot help it. I've been hurt, left behind, rejected, heartbroken and it is never something I ever want to feel again. When trusting God is the most terrifying route. ★GASP★ some of you right now are shaking your head, some of you may not ever have this problem (I commend you) and some of you are like "GIRL, I needed to hear this. I NEEDED to hear that I am not alone. I NEEDED to know that someone understands me and won't judge. No judgement here, not one. I don't want to be judged for doing this either". So what do I do about it, you ask? I know you've heard of the phrase "practice makes perfect", and that is exactly what I (we) need to do. Each and every time the shield of fear starts to come up, we have to quickly grab that shield of faith and hold on with dear life; I am convinced that every time we watch God prevail in protecting us, it will only get easier with each step forward. I am fighting the good fight with you, I am running this race with you sister. The coolest part of this; as scary and new as it may be at times, God will use it to GROW us through the process. TRUST HIM and your **confidence** and life will completely change for the absolute better. God never promises things will be easy, but He does say that it will be worth it. His way is the ONLY way to go, and it's the only way that we can be fully healed from our fears. Girl, you've got this; today is the day that you stand proud in the woman of Christ that you are, shoulders back and mind FULL of trust in that God will be your protector and regardless of what comes, He will never leave your side. In those moments, you don't have to be afraid anymore; He holds your heart and He's never letting go.

Faith before fear, faith before fear; say it with me, faith before fear. You go this girl, because remember that God always has your back.

CHAPTER NINE

PURITY & MODESTY

"And I want women to get in there with the men in humility before God, not primping before a mirror or chasing the latest fashions but doing something beautiful for God and becoming beautiful doing it"
1 Peter 2:9-10

Less is more. Show more skin. Reveal your cleavage. Wear shorter skirts. It's more important to be desired than to dress modestly. This chapter right here, is probably the one I am most passionate about. This is a topic that I am SURE that I will address in any type of speaking event with women I have that pertains to **confidence.** Being desired is an amazing thing, when you are desired by your husband in the bounds of marriage that Christ intended within His word. Ladies, not on social media, not when it's at the stake of someone else's husband noticing, and not by a total stranger that would rather meet you based on what he sees than what is within your heart. Women are not sex objects; although the world would press that to be true, you don't ever have to mistake that God isn't in that statement whole-heartedly.

Men are attracted to skin, they are visually made, and it doesn't change just because they get older. The Lord never stated that the male species would become blind of all other Women once the "I Do's" commence. It's how strong a man is in his faith and relationship with God that makes EVERY difference in the world. God created men this way so that they are to be utterly enamored with the bodies of their wives alone; although at a guys defense, society and this fallen world don't make it an easy street for them. This is why it is crucially important that we are consistently praying for our men. OR, if you are currently single, praying for your future husband is extremely important too!

Praying for their hearts, their relationships with God, the purity of their minds, thoughts and actions. Why would I start a chapter like this you ask? Well, why do women dress as they do? To get their OWN attention, I think not. There is definitely a level of **confidence** that a woman should have, but dressing less than modest; especially around younger generations of growing women in Christ, can set a completely wrong example. These young women are CRAVING for our example; truly, and they need to see that being modest and Christlike is an incredibly beautiful and respected thing.

Now, don't get me wrong, I am a 34 year old woman that loves getting my hair done, choosing fashions that fit my "classy hippie" style, making sure my nails are taken care of and working out to look better and FEEL better about myself. I don't believe in my heart that THIS is what God is speaking of when He says "primping before a mirror or chasing the latest fashions". God made us who we are, and we are FEARFULLY AND WONDERFULLY made; He desires for us to feel beautiful…..most importantly to

KNOW we are beautiful, and that isn't what is just displayed on the outside. He is speaking of our hearts. It becomes a sin only when our beauty and self-imagine become more important than God, and becoming everything that Christ has created us to individually be. We as Christian women (and non-christian alike) are bombarded like crazy with what is socially "acceptable" beauty. There are honestly times that it makes me nauseous thinking about the world that my 7 year old daughter is growing up in. The enemy is running rampant and it isn't going to get any better any time soon. Less is not more, MORE is more where modesty is concerned and it doesn't make us any less attractive to represent our status of Daughter of the King well. Makes us no better than anyone else, but we are held to a higher standard. I get it and understand it fully; we think that if we don't "look like so and so" or don't "wear things more revealing" that we just aren't beautiful or acceptable enough and that couldn't be any further from the truth. Raw, real and honest ladies; posting pictures of yourself with your cleavage and bodies hanging out ON PURPOSE is not what God has intended for a royal daughter. Think of it this way. I see picture after picture of the very beautiful Kate Middleton and Megan Markle; both now royalty, and completely stunning. They are as modest as it comes and it just flourishes into even more beauty when you see the way they carry themselves. They are of royal lineage now; just as YOU are within the Kingdom of God, so why should it be any different for us?

I struggled with this fact for many years, and I still struggle at times. You see, we think that teenage girls are the only ones who truly battle with self image and also representing who we are in Christ....WRONG! Women of ALL ages have these fears, these self image issues, this lacking of **confidence.** If you are reading this right now, there are women in your life or that you've seen that struggle severely with these very things & you wouldn't even know it! Total truth! I will always be raw and real, because sometimes it's exactly what someone needs to hear. Another woman's beauty does not subtract from our own, because there hasn't ever been another YOU created by God, EVER. You are you, and you are absolutely and undeniably gorgeous girl. I mean that with every beat of my heart! When we spend too much extra time worrying about what we look like as opposed to what God has for us to do to fulfill the purpose He has for us, it will almost always begin chipping away at our **confidence.** We will never go wrong when we turn it all over to Him, get lost in His unwavering love, and be committed to serving Him. It's in serving Him and serving others that our TRUE **confidence** and beauty emerges. You don't believe me, try it!! Try surrendering to God and serving others and try not to be full of joy, happiness and love. There are times that I forget who I am and Christ is always faithful in reminding me. In those moments He has me serving and taking my mind off myself; it's like I am receiving a breath of new life, like…."Ohh wow, Tiffany there you are! Where have you been" (Yes, I literally say that to myself….what can I say….I love talking out-loud to myself.) Let's not fool anyone, so do you!! The world pushes "sexy" and we as women of Christ are called to go against the "worldly" standard and bring out the "holy". I know I am not preaching to solely myself right now. Now, I am not speaking of being sexy as it pertains to marriage, your husband, etc. I am talking about bringing yourself DOWN to the world's idea of what that should be, and keeping yourself up here on the solid rock of modesty with Jesus.

CHAPTER TEN

"MISS CONGENIALITY"

"But The Lord replied to her by saying, Martha, you
are anxious and troubled about many things"
Luke 10:41

Now, all of us are blessed with talents; things that we are naturally good at and love to do. As women, we naturally gravitate toward the "doing" aspect of things, or as I like to call it "getting the job done". I personally don't enjoy having to wait on others to do what I know that I can do for myself. Now I admit that it's part of the way that I was brought up to be by my parents (independent and strong), part stubbornness, and then the biggest part being the servant's heart God has instilled within me. Okay; can I be honest? MAYBE it's the most stubborn part that oftentimes takes precedence over my servants heart. I naturally by nature do not like to ask for help and I pride myself in getting things done rather than procrastinating and leaving it for another day. It's a positive thing, but then it can also be a negative thing in my life when it comes to hearing from God and entering into that sacredness where He talks to me and builds my **confidence.**

We all know the story of Mary and Martha, found in Luke chapter 10, verses 38-42, and if you don't......allow me to make a short story shorter to explain the basis of what is going on. Jesus was traveling and ended up in a village on His journey and pays a visit to the home of Martha and her sister Mary. Now, Mary is so very EAGER to learn and immediately seats herself at the feet of Jesus; listening to His teachings. Now at the same time; my girl Martha is busy "doing" and "getting the job done" serving Jesus, and even goes as far as asking for "pity" from Jesus and requests that He asks her sister to help her! GIIIRRRRRLLLLL! This is a face slap moment. Jesus replies; not in the way Martha would think, but lets her know that she is too busy and just needs to RELAX. The growing and learning is not found in chores and serving in this moment, but listening and hearing from Jesus. There are Martha's in this world and then there are Mary's. Ladies, I am a Martha by nature; I'll admit it. I believe that the perfect balance would be to get to a place where we are a little bit of Martha AND a little bit of Mary; coinciding at the same time. Easier said that done for sure sometimes, right?

To show you just how BAD of a Martha I used to be; thank God I've grown since this particular time in my life. I seriously remember back when I was 22; I had just had my gallbladder removed laparoscopically (small incisions on my stomach), and within only a week I was trying to be back up and moving about doing house work. Keeping in mind that I was so extremely sore and could barely get out of bed on my own, but somehow I kept telling myself that "doing things" rather than resting was a better idea. I wasn't listening to my own body, let alone listening to God. I ended up ripping open one of my sutures a bit and was then FORCED to allow myself to heal; because if I hadn't, I would have bigger scars than I already have now (which are minimal, THANKFULLY!)

God's desire is for us to speak to Him, to Listen to Him and to follow Him; while at the same time taking what He teaches us and putting it into action. The key statement would be "putting it into action". We can speak to God and hear back from Him until we're blue in the face, but if we aren't putting His teachings into action, the enemy will be ALL over that. It would be like reading a recipe for a new dish that you are wanting to make (for me it would be to ATTEMPT to make), and after you read over the ingredients needed/directions, you move forward with trying to make the dish entirely yourself; completely disregarding what you just read in the directions. Not only would that be incorrect, it would potentially end up tasting horrible!! If you have the instruction right in front of you telling you exactly what to do (making it really easy on you), why is it that we choose to sometimes "go it alone" or end up "winging it"? I have done this, and too many times to count; thinking that somehow I know better.....I am with you girl! Satan KNOWS that if he can get you to that slippery slope of moving forward on full blast in one specific direction sweet Mary or Martha; never looking back, that you will begin to attempt to live within your OWN strength instead of utilizing the strength available to us through God. The kind of strength that keeps on giving, instead of depleting us of all energy and **confidence.** When we aren't obeying and listening to God; we are stunting our growth, and that is exactly the consistent motive of the enemy.

From the time I wake up in the morning, to the time I go to bed at night, I am constantly moving and doing something. My husband and daughter would be the first to tell you that I am always cleaning, serving, moving (I like to call it "shakin 'and bakin'", even though I'm never doing much baking at all, LOL!), and there are days that I honestly jump right into the craziness of the day before ever allowing myself to hear directly from God on exactly what He has planned for me to do on that particular day. These are the days that I can go, go, go all day long and by the end of the day

I am saying to myself "what exactly did I accomplish today"? Come on ladies, don't leave me hanging, there are some of you that know exactly what I am saying!! It is the most CONFUSING and FRUSTRATING lullaby to put you to sleep at night, LOL! I mean, really!

Being a "Miss Congeniality" can be all fine and dandy; but through what I've learned through God teaching me (being a Martha), I can go all day long.....but if I'm not giving myself that quiet time to hear from Him, I'm not growing. Likewise (if you are a Mary), hearing from Him, but never applying and moving, you aren't growing at the pace in which God desires. God's desire is ALWAYS that we reach our biggest and greatest potential as a Woman of Christ; He made us to be who we are for a reason, and our journey with Him is to find that healthy balance. Only Christ can lead us to that place, and it will always be within His strength and found in Him.

I want to share a little story with you; that just happened last week, and it was a teachable moment that God displayed what getting to that "perfect balance" looks like. I was getting ready to head to the store with my daughter, and my last step of getting ready is to put on my wedding ring and the rest of my jewelry. As I was putting on my ring, I heard the Lord whisper to my spirit "wear the pink band that says "BEAUTIFUL". So, I have this pink bracelet; made of the rubbery material that the WWJD bracelets are made from, and inscribed in black it says "BEAUTIFUL" & "Psalm 139:14 derived from the verse "You are fearfully and wonderfully made". It's a bracelet I'll wear from time to time, but I hadn't worn it in a while and God said CLEAR AS DAY that I needed to put it on. Now there are times that I hear from God, and then there are times that I HEAR FROM GOD!! This was one of those times that was completed unmistakable!! So, Anni and I leave for Walmart and as we are about to turn into the parking lot; I see a girl in an electric wheelchair on the sidewalk in front of the gas station next door to Walmart, and she's holding a sign that says "get cash now". She must have been working because she was also wearing a styrofoam hat that looked like the crown of the Statue of Liberty. Just as I'm looking over at her on the side of the road; God speaks to me, and He says to me "I want you to give the bracelet to that girl". I couldn't back out of this one ladies, I heard Him too loud and clear that I couldn't just excuse it for just being my own voice inside my head. So, I pulled into the gas station and walked up to the girl, and just as soon as I got over to her, the wind began to blow her hat off.....if I hadn't been there in that EXACT moment, she would have completely lost her hat to the wind. GOD WAS TOTALLY SHOWING OFF at that point, making it completely obvious to me; reminding me that He is in control, and that He had me placed there at exactly the right time. I bent down in front of her and introduced myself and I asked her, her name and she told me "Desiree". I said "It's so nice to meet you Desiree! I was leaving the house today and God spoke to me about wearing this bracelet (I took it off to show her) and it says "BEAUTIFUL". It's taken from the verse Psalm 139:14 that you are fearfully and wonderfully made. You are so beautiful and loved by God and He wanted you to know that today. I want you to have this (and I then helped her put it on" She smiled SO BIG and said

"Thank you so much!" I told her she was so welcome and that I hoped she had a great rest of her day. As I was walking back to the Jeep, my eyes started welling up with tears; because just as much as it blessed Desiree, it blessed me so much more!! God wanted Desiree to know just how beautiful she was and how much He loves her; help her to regain some of the **confidence** she may have been lacking, and to bless her in the way that He knew she needed in that moment!!

I couldn't help but think, if I hadn't gotten up that morning to put God first by starting my day out with reading in The Word, talking with Him, praying, and asking Him to use me to bless someone that day; would it still have happened the way that it did? I gave God my "Mary" time and I chose to also put my "Martha" in action, and what He did was show me that it was exactly what I needed to be growing. The ways He wants to use me are only possible by allowing Him to lead me, teach me and asking Him to help me apply it to my own life; THIS ladies, is how you GROW. It was a tremendous learning experience for me, but at the same time a HUGE reminder that God is in control and we don't have to try and achieve this perfect balance without His help. Trying to do it all seems heroic to us women at times, and completely necessary....I feel this way at times still too, but God always quickly reminds me when it's time to find that balance again. With me, it's always that I start doing too much and I am not doing enough listening, and acts without proper instruction can make me feel like I am running around like a chicken with my head cut off. Just as doing too much listening and not enough applying through action can lead to that lonely idle feeling, like you aren't moving forward day to day and always leaves you wondering why.....feeling discontent.

So I ask you to ask God today, am I a Mary or am I a Martha, OR am I that perfect balance of both. By the way, if you are the perfect balance of both, God bless your heart, truly!

These are questions/prayers I ask and pray to God frequently during my daily devotion, bible reading & prayer times:

-God how can I continue to grow from where I am

now?

-What things within my life and daily routine might be hindering me from growth currently?

-I need to hear from you more, God, what can I do to remove the anxious anxieties so that I can hear you more clearly and regain complete **confidence?**

-Lord, help me to get to a place (with your leading) that I can begin to have a healthy balance of both Mary and Martha.

-God, I ask for your leading in applying your teachings to my life.

-God, how can you use me today to bless someone else's life for your glory?

Always remember my sweet Mary & Martha's; you are who you are for a reason, and that reason is that this world wouldn't ever be the same without you being in it. You are indeed "Fearfully and Wonderfully Made"!! Our own personal journey with God in growing is so beautiful and I hope that now you feel better understood and also a sense of hope about how to keep moving forward in that growth to become every single ounce of that Woman of God you've been created to be!! BOOM!!

CHAPTER ELEVEN

SOCIAL MEDIA

*"Cultivate inner beauty, the gentle, gracious kind that
God delights in. The holy women of old were
beautiful before God that way, and were good, loyal
wives to their husbands. Sarah, for instance, taking care
of Abraham, would address him as "my dear husband."
You'll be true daughters of Sarah if you do the same,
un-anxious and unintimidated"*

1 Peter 3:3-6

Facebook. Twitter. Instagram. Snapchat. and because I am getting a little older; I am not completely up to "the times" with all the thousands of additional sources our generation utilizes today. Some would refer to them as "the fabric of our lives", but as I recall, at one time that was cotton......there was actually a commercial with music and everything. Now, the standard in which a lot of women live their lives is led by what the world is saying should be the "norm", completely opposite of what God teaches through His Word.

There are literally a million and one different types of social media apps being downloaded on the daily. I honestly couldn't have written this book without including this chapter, and that fact truly makes me cringe a bit. I feel so blessed that; even at the young age of 33 (hehe), I was privileged enough to have grown up in an era without iPhones, apps and social media all together; it was a REFRESHING time. I spent my time enjoying nature, riding peddle bikes around the small city of Oxford, Michigan with my brother from dawn till dusk. I am so "old-school" that I cannot even fully explain it to you. Social Media; as time goes on especially, annoys me.....and I truly believe as a Christian Woman....it should you too at times. It's frightening to stop and think about what teenage girls are witnessing today through Facebook, Instagram, Twitter, Snapchat and whatever else there may be (I know there are a million other apps they use today). I have a 7 year old daughter, a 21 year old stepdaughter and a 19 year old stepson, and it is scary having them grow up in a society that; to me in my younger years, would have been completely ruined by. My husband and I travel the country 9 months out of the year speaking to Middle school and High school kids about these very things! There are young teenage girls feeling bombarded and made to feel like they HAVE to post pictures of themselves nude to get any kind of attention from a boy. UGH! It is not only disgusting, but it is NOT what God desires for any of us; because I know there are grown men that do the same thing. I told you ladies, I am raw and real and I won't hold back because this is beyond serious. Ladies, protect your eyes and your heart on social media, and I am praying this very thing as I am writing this RIGHT NOW. If you have daughters, nieces, any younger girls in your life that consider you a mentor; PROTECT THEM, because it's only going to get worse. It's so easy to fall susceptible, even as adult women; the enemy wants you to find that life enticing; when all it brings is destruction. Your **confidence,** salvation and self-worth is NOT found in another Woman's picture of her FILTERED "seemingly perfect" body. In today's society it's somehow become more influential to have beautiful (EDITED) pictures on Instagram, then it is to be a true beauty within your heart; having a servant's heart towards others. I feel like our Heavenly Father is right "upstairs" staring down at us and literally pulling out his hair. This means that your worth doesn't involve a tutorial on "how to look more like a Kardashian or a never-ending competition with your neighbor regarding who most resembles being "the or "perfect Mom" on your respective pages or news feeds. No, no, no dear Princess, your beauty is and SHOULD be found in Jesus alone; He is your creator. You can be the most beautiful "put together" woman in the world, but if your insides aren't matching your outsides, you aren't anything but the creaking of a rusty gate......

*"If I speak with human eloquence and angelic
ecstasy but don't love, I'm nothing but the
creaking of a rusty gate"*
1 Corinthians 13: 1

I can assure you that God never intended our lives to be dictated through a technological application on a tiny portable phone; what He intended is so much more, than in the midst of these things, we be the "salt and light" of the world. While other Women are posting "clefie" photos of themselves (that being cleavage selfies), or even to the point that with one quick swift yank of the blanket or cover-up; they'd be naked, we as Women of Christ are held to a higher standard. We HAVE to be. I CANNOT SAY THIS ENOUGH! We have to be on top of this ladies, there are young women watching us and depending on us to be making the right decisions!! Keeping ourselves deep in God's Word; absorbing the scripture daily, is the only thing that will keep us on track. On the contrary, giving into the world and living/posting just as everyone else does, will only bring a deeper seeded need for validation, and have to doing things that could quite possibly make you ashamed to admit you've done. It can actually take away your **confidence**. So, Sister; I say this with the complete utmost respect, if you are posting "clefie" pictures or pictures pointing to anything remotely close to nudity or needing validation for self-worth, I ask you to pray over that situation and listening to what God places on your heart. I follow the general rule in my own life that if my husband wouldn't want me posting it or if my daughters wouldn't be proud of me posting it and MOST IMPORTANTLY what would God feel about me posting it, I don't post it. The world "seeing you" and all your skin will not give you **confidence**, it will leave you empty in the end or worse, headed down a path that you most likely don't want to be on, and according to The Bible; displeasing completely to our Heavenly Father.

Social Media can be such a positive thing, when used properly. It keeps us in touch with friends and family we don't normally see, can be a great start for a home business, and the resources go on and on. I don't believe God ever intended it to become anything other than a GOOD thing, and yet it keeps being used in less than impactful ways. Ladies, let us stand up and fight for what we believe and show this generation that being Godly online is so much more fulfilling than using it for personal unclean gain. No one else may see what you are up to most of the time when on social media; but God does, and He is looking for you to change the standards and raise that bar up high girl! Concentrating on growing our inner beauty just as much; if not MORE, as our outer appearance. AMEN!

CHAPTER TWELVE

REACH OUT

"For where two or three gather in my name,
there I am with them."
Matthew 18:20

Have you ever stopped and just observed the mannerisms of a roly-poly? The way those teeny tiny little bugs can go from walking to "balling" (my own personal definition of course) in a matter of just a few seconds? Okay, bear with me…..there is a method to my madness. Some of you know exactly what I am speaking of, others' may not have the slightest idea. So, let me explain. The roly-poly is a tiny little gray bug; with a tiny body that resembles a turtle shell almost (without the hard toughness), and teeny little feeler legs that go on for days. When the opportunity strikes and these little guys feel threatened in any way, that roll up into a tiny ball that encloses their feet and underbelly completely; they are no bigger than your finger tip. I remember growing up, my brother and I would sit in the dirt for hours and simply tap their tiny little backs; just to see how many we could force to roll-up. I just remember watching and thinking, how cool is that? They feel threatened or unsociable and they roll right up into a ball in-turn protecting themselves from the entire outside world. It is their instinctive way.

I don't know about you, but there have been numerous instances when I've been torn down, felt threatened, lacked complete **confidence** and been defeated, and in most cases; my first reaction is to become a recluse. Get myself as far away humanly possible from the chaos and force those degrading thoughts; demanding my attention and emotions, to vanish from my mind.....if only for a little while. It is an instinct of protection and a place that we can travel for regeneration. I am half introvert and half extrovert and the way I unwind and regenerate is to pop in my earbuds, throw on some worship music and just soak it in. Small trips to this "vacation" spot in our mind can be beneficial, but if you aren't careful; it can be a festering ground for the enemy's lies. You see; the enemy hates, HATES, unity; especially among Christian Women, and as long as he can keep you singled out and down for the count, he knows you will resist growing closer to God. This is a specific area that the enemy targets most often in my own personal life, and if I had to make a bet; it would be for you too. As a Christian Woman, a Daughter of The King, a POWERHOUSE for Jesus; you are powerful, and GIRL…..don't even get me started on talking about the power that is present when two or MORE Christian women come together in prayer to represent one of their own fellow ladies in resisting the enemy. WOOOOOOO! There are literally demons shaking somewhere in this moment as I am typing these very words. The second a group of ladies join hands and all resound in the phrase "Heavenly Father, in Jesus name", it's ALL over!! The enemy stands zero chance when you reach out to others. I'm not just talking about just ANY type of person(s), I'm talking about your Christian mentors and fellow sisters in Christ, that desire nothing more than to continually watch you grow into the **confidence** of who God created you to be and be so blessed in your life by your mighty King!! In Jesus name, can I get an AMEN!

Little side note; I'm currently sitting on a 2 1/2 hour flight to Dallas, Texas, in the very back row of the plane, with my Husband's head lying on the tip of my shoulder, and smiling from ear to ear. I love making the enemy furious; and you should too, he wants to destroy you, your life and keep you isolated permanently. Keep your Christian girlfriends on speed dial, stay in touch with them frequently and if you are a Christian woman who doesn't honestly have Christian friends that resemble this definition; REACH OUT, and ask God to lead the way. I can promise you that you won't be disappointed. Ladies, we need to have accountability partners just as much as the Christian Men in our lives, and we all sometimes need to be reminded of the way home, and these beautiful ladies in Christ lead us back into the arms of Jesus. I have two very best friends; their names are Kari and Julie, and I love these women! HI GIRLS! Not only are they amazing friends to me, but they love Jesus and aren't afraid to "give it to me straight". I never have to worry about them NOT being there for me, not leading me to Jesus, and not laying it out on the table for me if something I am saying or doing might not be good for me or in alignment with what God has for me. I prayed for many years that God would bring women like them into my life, and it is such a blessing. When you have other women in Christ; like this that God brings to you, it is beyond refreshing to be able to talk with them about any issues and have **confidence** that they will lead you in the direction of Jesus. There isn't anything Satan can do when women come together and pray over one another in love and for each other's best interests.

No matter how much it hurts, or the content within the enemies whispers telling you "They couldn't care less about what you are going through, why even bother?" (sound familiar?), it is imperative that you push through and remain connected. The enemy wants you to feel alone, like no one resonates; it is in that place that he can destroy you and depression strikes. Yes, I said DESTROY; you don't believe me, read it for yourself: *"Be alert and of sober mind. Your enemy the devil prowls around like a roaring lion looking for someone to devour" 1 Peter 5:8.* Nothing says it better than God's Word. It's like the kid in gym class that always gets picked last, no one really wants to be alone. God already has women lined up for you ladies; women you'll meet over the course of your life that will change your outlook and help you grow, and it's incredible when you have those kindred spirits with the women you consider your best friends!!

CHAPTER THIRTEEN

GOD LOVES YOU!

"I'm absolutely convinced that nothing, nothing living or dead, angelic or demonic, today or tomorrow, high or low, thinkable or unthinkable, absolutely nothing can get between us and God's love because of the way that Jesus our Master has embraced us."

Romans 8:38-39

Here we are; the last chapter, and I've saved the absolute **BEST** for last.

We have been conditioned by the world and society today that love; in its truest form, is not only CONDITIONAL but also that something that is to be earned. Basically, "I'll love you and respect you just as long as it is benefiting me. That "one for you, one for me" mentality. The act of caring genuinely or giving selflessly to someone else is completely non-existent with this impossible distorted definition. God's definition and example couldn't be further from this. In fact, God has stated that there isn't anything, and I mean ANYTHING that we could think, say or do that could ever separate us from His love. The actual realization of this should help in restoring any absent **confidence** that may be plaguing your heart in this very moment. I don't know about you, but I'm calling the world's/society bluff! Do me a HUGE favor, and take a moment to read 1 Corinthians 13:4-7 & 13 below; really BREATHE it in with every word, let it engulf the depths of your soul and replenish the most hollow parts of your beating heart.

"Love is patient, love is kind, it does not envy, it does not boast. It is not proud, it is not rude, it is not self-seeking. It is not easily angered, it keeps no record of wrongs. Love does not delight in evil, but rejoices with the truth, it always protects, always trusts, always hopes, always perseveres, and

now these three remain; faith, hope and love, but the greatest of these is love"

God has put on my spirit to expand on this scripture for you:

Love is **PATIENT**- Patience in definition is "The capacity to accept or tolerate delay, trouble, or suffering without getting angry or upset. UMM, did you get that last part? "Suffering without getting angry or upset" Honestly, that part made me cringe a bit, but not in the worst way. Patience is a BEAUTIFUL thing when it comes to love. This is how God loves us so patiently and how he desires us to love others. Some individuals are much more patient than others; but rest assured if you need more patience, all you have to do is pray for it…..but it just might require you "suffering without getting angry or upset". Think about a time that a loved one, friend, coworker reacted in a patient way with you, instead of a very angry or resentful way; when that is what you were expecting. How did it make you feel? It most likely calmed your heart, validated your feelings and made you feel LOVED.

Love is **KIND**- Regardless of what we say or do, God always comes at us with kindness, always. He desires for us to always be kind to others, in the way we'd want to be treated. He is so good to us, and kindness is His character. Be kind to others, ask God to help you LOVE with kindness in the way that He does. It's love at its truest.

Love does not **ENVY**- Envy means a feeling of disconnect or resentful longing aroused by someone else's possessions, qualities or luck. When we love someone, we love them for who they are and we are excited for them when they have victories and triumphs, not pushing them away or reacting in jealousy because it's something WE want. God loves us so well, with no disconnect or resentful feelings. God calls us to love others for everything they are and accepting how God blesses them, He wants to bless you too!!

Love does not **BOAST**- Boasting by definition is to talk with excessive pride and self-satisfaction about your achievements, possessions or abilities. Talk about God wanting us to be humble! What we do in private will be brought to the forefront by God when it's time. God doesn't call us to "toot our own horns" because He promises to be our validator.

Love is not ***PROUD***- Love is not arrogant or full of self-pride. God loves us so freely without expecting anything in return, that's His kind of love.

Love always protects others, trusts, hopes and never gives up. God leaves the 99 to come to find us each and every time we need Him. God IS love. Above all things, everything, He loves us!!

Love isn't just an intense feeling of deep affection; but it goes so much deeper than that, it's the most spectacular and indescribable deep euphoric feeling toward another human being…..even Webster's Dictionary knows that. God isn't just some horrible condemning ruler; sitting above, and watching our every move to point out every fault and weakness; He is HEAVENLY, and He loves us in such an outstandingly pure way. He loves you when you are happy, He loves you when you are sad, He loves you when you are angry and even screaming at the top of your lungs. I am talking real, raw, honest and true here. Things that you've thought, words that you've spoken and actions you've taken that you are guilt stricken and ashamed of (some of them maybe only God being aware of). God sees you in your darkest (no so admirable moments, and yes we all have them....you are not alone). You cannot hide your face from God; He loves you, and loves you in ALL of your forms. In those moments when you've acted a complete fool and you don't know how anyone could ever remotely forgive and accept you once again; those are the moments He loves you the most, and condemnation is the furthest thing He desires you to feel. I mean think about this, REALLY think about it; it brings tears to my eyes just attempting to fathom the depths of His love for us. He breaks our hearts for what breaks His, but when our hearts are broken; He is quick to be closer to mend and repair, restoring **confidence** within us of our value, His grace and His forgiveness. God's love has humbled me in ways that have been life-changing, and the more understanding that I have of His character; the more I am in awe of Him.

Princess, our God has placed within you, priceless treasures and endless talents; you are a miraculous creation, one in a million. There won't ever be another YOU. He looks at your sweet face with adoring love and affection and He is so proud of how far you've come and He wants you to be EXCITED for where He is taking you next, total truth! It doesn't matter who you are, the **confidence** of the woman that you are is ready to shine COMPLETELY through. You are a POWERHOUSE in Christ, you OWN power through His name and He wants you to use it. We are held to a higher standard as Women in Christ and there are others' looking at us and watching us in our journey along the way, they WANT and NEED to see us rocking-it-out. You were chosen before you ever KNEW God had hand-picked you.

Rise Up!! Rise Up!!

YOU, the <u>Powerhouse Woman of God</u> and rock-out-that-**CONFIDENCE**!! BOOM!!

www.ingramcontent.com/pod-product-compliance
Lightning Source LLC
Chambersburg PA
CBHW060054100426
42742CB00014B/2831